I0428391

Problem-Oriented Guides for Police
Problem-Solving Tools Series
No. 1

Assessing Responses to Problems: An Introductory Guide for Police Problem Solvers

Contents

Figures

Tables

About the Problem-Solving Tools Series

The *Problem-Solving Tools* are one of three series of the *Problem-Oriented Guides for Police.* The other two are the *Problem-Specific Guides* and *Response Guides.*

The *Problem-Oriented Guides for Police* summarize knowledge about how police can reduce the harm caused by specific crime and disorder problems. They are guides to preventing problems and improving overall incident response, not to investigating offenses or handling specific incidents. Neither do they cover all of the technical details about how to implement specific responses. The guides are written for police—of whatever rank or assignment—who must address the specific problems the guides cover. The guides will be most useful to officers who:

- Understand basic problem-oriented policing principles and methods
- Can look at problems in depth
- Are willing to consider new ways of doing police business
- Understand the value and the limits of research knowledge
- Are willing to work with other community agencies to find effective solutions to problems

The *Problem-Solving Tools* summarize knowledge about information gathering and analysis techniques that might assist police at any of the four main stages of a problem-oriented project: scanning, analysis, response, and assessment. Each guide:

- Describes the kind of information produced by each technique
- Discusses how the information could be useful in problem-solving
- Gives examples of previous uses of the technique
- Provides practical guidance about adapting the technique to specific problems
- Provides templates of data collection instruments (where appropriate)
- Suggests how to analyze data gathered by using the technique
- Shows how to interpret the information correctly and present it effectively
- Warns about any ethical problems in using the technique
- Discusses the limitations of the technique when used by police in a problem-oriented project
- Provides reference sources of more detailed information about the technique
- Indicates when police should seek expert help in using the technique

Extensive technical and scientific literature covers each technique addressed in the *Problem-Solving Tools*. The guides aim to provide only enough information about each technique to enable police and others to use it in the course of problem-solving. In most cases, the information gathered during a problem-solving project does not have to withstand rigorous scientific scrutiny. Where police need greater confidence in the data, they might need expert help in using the technique. This can often be found in local university departments of sociology, psychology, and criminal justice.

The information needs for any single project can be quite diverse, and it will often be necessary to use a variety of data collection techniques to meet those needs. Similarly, a variety of different analytic techniques may be needed to analyze the data. Police and crime analysts may be unfamiliar with some of the techniques, but the effort invested in learning to use them can make all the difference to the success of a project.

The COPS Office defines community policing as "a philosophy that promotes organizational strategies, which support the systematic use of partnerships and problem-solving techniques, to proactively address the immediate conditions that give rise to public safety issues such as crime, social disorder, and fear of crime." These guides emphasize *problem-solving* and *police-community partnerships* in the context of addressing specific public safety problems. For the most part, the organizational strategies that can facilitate problem-solving and police-community partnerships vary considerably and discussion of them is beyond the scope of these guides.

These guides have drawn on research findings and police practices in the United States, the United Kingdom, Canada, Australia, New Zealand, the Netherlands, and Scandinavia. Even though laws, customs and police practices vary from country to country, it is apparent that the police everywhere experience common problems. In a world that is becoming increasingly interconnected, it is important that police be aware of research and successful practices beyond the borders of their own countries.

Each guide is informed by a thorough review of the research literature and reported police practice, and each guide is anonymously peer-reviewed by a line police officer, a police executive and a researcher prior to publication. The review process is independently managed by the COPS Office, which solicits the reviews.

For more information about problem-oriented policing, visit the Center for Problem-Oriented Policing online at www.popcenter.org. This website offers free online access to:

- The *Problem-Specific Guides* series
- The companion *Response Guides* and *Problem-Solving Tools* series
- Special publications on crime analysis and on policing terrorism
- Instructional information about problem-oriented policing and related topics
- An interactive problem-oriented policing training exercise
- An interactive *Problem Analysis Module*
- Online access to important police research and practices
- Information about problem-oriented policing conferences and award programs

Acknowledgments

The Problem-Oriented Guides for Police are produced by the Center for Problem-Oriented Policing, whose officers are Michael S. Scott (Director), Ronald V. Clarke (Associate Director), and Graeme R. Newman (Associate Director). While each guide has a primary author, other project team members, COPS Office staff, and anonymous peer reviewers contributed to each guide by proposing text, recommending research and offering suggestions on matters of format and style.

The project team that developed the guide series comprised Herman Goldstein (University of Wisconsin Law School), Ronald V. Clarke (Rutgers University), John E. Eck (University of Cincinnati), Michael S. Scott (University of Wisconsin Law School), Rana Sampson (Police Consultant), and Deborah Lamm Weisel (North Carolina State University).

Karin Schmerler, Rita Varano, and Nancy Leach oversaw the project for the COPS Office. Suzanne Fregly edited the guides. Research for the guides was conducted at the Criminal Justice Library at Rutgers University under the direction of Phyllis Schultze.

The project team also wishes to acknowledge the members of the San Diego, National City, and Savannah police departments who provided feedback on the guides' format and style in the early stages of the project, as well as the line police officers, police executives, and researchers who peer reviewed each guide.

Introduction

The purpose of assessing a problem-solving effort is to help you make better decisions by answering two specific questions. First, did the problem decline? Answering this question helps you decide whether to end the problem-solving effort and focus resources on other problems. Second, if the problem did decline, did the response cause the decline? Answering this question helps you decide whether to apply the response to similar problems.

What This Guide Is About

This introduction to problem-solving assessments is intended to help you design evaluations to answer the two questions above. It was written for those who are responsible for evaluating the effectiveness of responses to problems, and who have a basic understanding of problem-oriented policing and the problem-solving process. This guide assumes a basic understanding of the SARA problem-solving process (scanning, analysis, response, and assessment), but it requires little or no experience with assessing problem solutions.

This guide was written based on the assumption that you have no outside assistance. Nevertheless, you should seek the advice and help of researchers with training and experience in evaluation, particularly if the problem you are addressing is large and complex. Requesting aid from an independent outside evaluator can be particularly helpful if there is controversy over a response's usefulness. Local colleges and universities are a good source for such expertise. Many social science departments—economics, political science, sociology, psychology, and criminal justice/criminology—have faculty and graduate students who are knowledgeable in program evaluation and related topics.

This guide is a companion reference to the *Problem-Oriented Guides for Police* series. Each guide in the series suggests ways to measure a particular problem, and describes possible responses to it. Though the evaluation principles discussed here are intended to apply to the specific problems in the guides, you should be able to apply them to any problem-solving project.

This is an introduction to a complex subject, and it emphasizes evaluation methods that are the most relevant to problem-oriented policing.[†] You should consult the list of recommended readings at the end of the guide if you are interested in exploring the topic of evaluation in greater detail.

Assessment and Decision Making

As stated, this guide is about aiding decision making. There are two key decisions to make regarding any problem-solving effort. First, did the problem decline enough for you to end the effort and apply resources elsewhere? If the problem did not decline substantially, then the job is not done. In such a case, the most appropriate decision may be to reanalyze the problem and develop a new response. Second, if the problem did decline substantially, then it might be worthwhile to apply the response to similar problems.

This guide focuses on the first decision—whether to end the problem-solving effort. The second decision has to do with future response applications. If the problem declined substantially, and if the response at least partly caused the decline, then you might consider using the response with other problems. But if the problem did not decline, or if it got worse, and this was due to an ineffective response, then future problem solvers should be alerted so they can develop better responses to similar problems. Future decisions about whether to use the response depend in part on assessment information. In this regard, assessment is an essential part of police organizational learning. Without assessments, problem solvers are constantly reinventing the wheel, and run the risk of repeating the same mistakes. Nevertheless, obtaining valid information to aid in decision making increases the complexity of assessments.

Making either decision requires a detailed understanding of the problem, of how the response is supposed to reduce the problem, and of the context in which the response has been implemented.[1] For this reason, the evaluation process begins after it is identified in the scanning stage.

This guide discusses two simple designs—pre-post and interrupted time series. The pre-post design is useful in making only the first type of decision—whether to end the problem-solving effort. The time series design can aid in making both types of decisions.

---

† Excluded from this discussion is any mention of significance testing and statistical estimation. Though useful methods, they cannot be described in a guide of this length sufficiently enough for you to effectively use them.

Finally, it is worth mentioning how the guide is organized. The body of the text addresses fundamental issues in constructing simple but useful evaluations. The endnotes provide a link to more-technical books on evaluation. Many of these clarify terminology. The appendixes expand on material in the text. Appendix A uses an extended example to show why evaluating responses over longer periods provides a better understanding of response effectiveness. Appendix B describes two advanced designs involving comparison (or "control" groups). Appendix C explains how to calculate a response's net effect on a problem. Appendix D provides a summary of the designs' strengths and weaknesses. Finally, Appendix E provides a checklist for going through the evaluation process, selecting the most applicable design, and drawing reasonable conclusions from evaluation results. You should read the body of the text before examining the appendixes.

In summary, this guide explains, in ordinary language, those aspects of evaluation methods that are most important to police when addressing problems. In the next section, we will examine how evaluation fits within the SARA problem-solving process. We will then examine the two major types of evaluation—process and impact.

Evaluation's Role in Problem Solving

It is important to distinguish between evaluation and assessment. Evaluation is scientific process for determining if a problem declined and if the solution caused the decline. As we will see, it begins at the moment the problem-solving process begins and continues through the completion of the effort. Assessment occurs at the final stage in the SARA problem-solving process.[2] It is the culmination of the evaluation process, the time when you draw conclusions about the problem and its solutions.

Though assessment is the final stage of both evaluation and problem solving, critical decisions about the evaluation are made throughout the process, as indicated in Figure 1. The left side shows the standard SARA process and some of the most basic questions asked at each stage. It also draws attention to the fact that the assessment may produce information requiring the problem solver to go back to earlier stages to make modifications. This is particularly the case if the response was not as successful as expected.

The right side of Figure 1 lists critical questions to address to conduct an evaluation. During the scanning stage, you must define the problem with sufficient precision to measure it. You will collect baseline data on the nature and scope of the problem during the analysis phase. Virtually every important question to be addressed during analysis will be important during assessment. This is because, during assessment, you want to know if the problem has changed. So data uncovered during analysis become vital baseline information (or "pre-response measures") during assessment.

Figure 1. The problem-solving process and evaluation

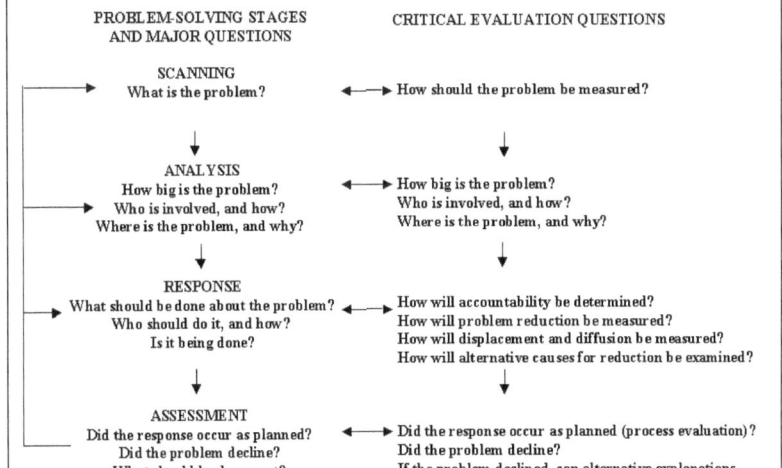

During the response stage, while developing a strategy to reduce the problem, you should also develop an accountability mechanism to be sure the various participants in the response do what they should be doing. As we will see later, one type of evaluation—process—is closely tied to accountability. Thus, while developing a response, it is important to determine how to assess accountability. Also, the type of response has a major influence on how you design the other type of evaluation—impact.

During assessment, you answer the following questions: Did the response occur as planned? Did the problem decline? If so, are there good reasons to believe the decline resulted from the response?

In summary, you begin planning for an evaluation when you take on a problem. The evaluation builds throughout the SARA process, culminates during the assessment, and provides findings that help you determine if you should revisit earlier stages to improve the response. You can use the checklist in Appendix E as a general guide to evaluation throughout the SARA process.

Types of Evaluations

There are two types of evaluations. You should conduct both. As we will see later, they complement each other.

Process Evaluations

Process evaluations ask the following questions: Did the response occur as planned? Did all the response components work? Or, stated more bluntly, Did you do what you said you would do? This is a question of accountability.

Let's start with a hypothetical example. A problem-solving team, after a careful analysis, determines that, to curb a street prostitution problem, they will ask the city's traffic engineering department to make a major thoroughfare one-way, and to create several dead-end streets to thwart cruising by "johns." This will be done immediately after a comprehensive crackdown on the prostitutes in the target area. Convicted prostitutes will be given probation under the condition that they do not enter the target area for a year. Finally, a nonprofit organization will help prostitutes who want to leave their line of work gain the necessary skills for legitimate employment. The vice squad, district patrol officers, prosecutor, local judges, probation office, sheriff's department, traffic engineering department, and nonprofit organization all agree to this plan.

A process evaluation will determine whether the crackdown occurred and, if so, how many arrests police made; whether the traffic engineering department altered street patterns as planned; and how many prostitutes asked for job skills assistance and found legitimate employment. The process evaluation will also examine whether everything occurred in the planned sequence. If you find that the crackdown occurred after the street alterations, that the police arrested only a fraction of the prostitutes, and that none of the prostitutes sought job skills, then you will suspect that the plan was not fully carried out, nor was it carried out in the specified sequence. You might conclude that the response was a colossal failure. However, the evidence provided gives us no indication of success or failure, because a process evaluation does not answer the question, What happened to the problem?

Impact Evaluations

To determine what happened to the problem, you need an impact evaluation. An impact evaluation asks the following questions: Did the problem decline? If so, did the response cause the decline? Continuing with our prostitution example, let's look at how it might work. During the analysis stage of the problem-solving process, patrol officers and vice detectives conduct a census of prostitutes operating in the target area. They also ask the traffic engineering department to install traffic counters on the major thoroughfare and critical side streets to measure traffic flow. This is done to determine how customers move through the area. The vice squad makes covert video recordings of the target area to document how prostitutes interact with potential customers. All of this is done before the problem-solving team selects a response, and the information gained helps the team to do so.

After the response is implemented (though not the planned response, as we have seen), the team decides to repeat these measures to see if the problem has declined. They discover that instead of the 23 prostitutes counted in the first census, only 10 can be found. They also find that there has been a slight decline in traffic on the major thoroughfare on Friday and Saturday nights, but not at other times. However, there has been a substantial decline in side street traffic on Friday and Saturday nights. New covert video recordings show that prostitutes in the area have changed how they approach vehicles, and are acting more cautiously. In short, the team has evidence that the problem has declined after response implementation.

So what has caused the problem to decline? You may be tempted to jump right into trying to answer this question, because it will help you determine if you can attribute the decline to the response. However, this question may not be as important as it first appears. After all, if the goal is to reduce or eliminate the problem, and this occurs, what difference does it make what the cause is? The answer is that it does not matter in the least, *unless* you are interested in using the same response for similar problems. If you have no interest in using the response again, then all that matters is that you have achieved the goal. You can then use the resources devoted to addressing the problem on some more pressing concern. But if you believe you can use the response again, it is very important to determine if the response caused the decline in the problem.

Let's assume the prostitution problem-solving team believes the response might be useful for addressing similar problems. The response, though not implemented according to plan, might have caused the decline, but it is also possible that something else caused the decline. There are two reasons the team takes this second possibility seriously. First, the actual response was somewhat haphazard, unlike the planned response. If the planned response had been implemented, the team would have a plausible explanation for the decline. But the jury-rigged nature of the actual response makes it a far less plausible explanation for the decline. Second, the impact evaluation is not particularly strong. Later, we will discuss why this is a weak evaluation, and what can be done to strengthen it.

Interpretation of Process and Impact Evaluations

Process and impact evaluations answer different questions, so their combined results are often highly informative. Table 1 summarizes the information you can glean from both evaluations. As you will see in Appendix E, the interpretation of this table depends on the type of design used for the impact evaluation. For the moment, however, we will assume that the evaluation design can show whether the response caused the problem to decline.

When a response is implemented as planned (or nearly so), the conclusions are much easier to interpret (cells A and B). When the response is not implemented as planned, we have more difficulty determining what happened, and what to do next (cells C and D). Cell D is particularly troublesome because all you really know is that "we did not do it, and it did not work." Should you try to implement your original plan, or should you start over from scratch?

Outcomes that fall into cell C merit further discussion. The decline in the problem means that you could end the problem-solving process and go on to something else. If the problem has declined considerably, this might be satisfactory. If, however, the problem is still too big, then you do not know whether to continue or increase the response (on the assumption that it is working, but more is needed). Alternatively, you could seek a different response (on the assumption that the response is not working, and something else is needed). In addition, you do not know if the response will be useful for similar problems. In short, it is difficult to replicate successes when you do not know why you were successful. The basic lesson is that all assessments should contain both a process and an impact evaluation.

Table 1. Interpreting results of process and impact evaluations

		Process Evaluation Results	
		Response implemented as planned, or nearly so	Response not implemented, or implemented in a radically different manner than planned
Impact Evaluation Results	Problem declined	**A.** Evidence that the response caused the decline	**C.** Suggests that other factors may have caused the decline, or that the response was accidentally effective
	Problem did not decline	**B.** Evidence that the response was ineffective, and that a different response should be tried	**D.** Little is learned. Perhaps if the response had been implemented as planned, the problem would have declined, but this is speculative

A process evaluation involves comparing the planned response with what actually occurred. Much of this information becomes apparent while managing a problem-solving process. If the vice squad is supposed to arrest prostitutes in the target area, you can determine whether they have from departmental records and discussions with squad members. There will be judgment calls, nevertheless. For example, how many arrests are required? The response plan may call for the arrest of 75 percent of the prostitutes, but only 60 percent are arrested. Whether this is a serious violation of the plan may be difficult to determine. Much of a process evaluation is descriptive (these people did these things, in this order, using these procedures). Nevertheless, numbers can help. In our example, data on traffic volume show where street alterations have changed driving patterns, and these pattern changes are consistent with what was anticipated in the response plan.

In short, a process evaluation tells what happened, when, and to whom. Though it does not tell whether the response affected the problem, it is very useful for determining how to interpret impact evaluation results.

Conducting Impact Evaluations

There are two parts to impact evaluations. The first involves measuring the problem. The second involves systematically comparing changes in measures, using an evaluation design. Evaluation designs are created to provide the maximum evidence that the response was the primary cause of the change in the measure. Weak designs may be adequate for demonstrating that the problem declined, but they provide little assurance that the response caused the decline. Strong designs provide much greater assurance that the response caused the decline.

Measures

Impact evaluations require measures of the problem before and after the response. You should start deciding how to measure the problem during the scanning stage, and have made final decisions about measures by the time you have completed the analysis. This will allow you to use information collected during the analysis to describe the problem before the response. During the assessment stage, you take measures of the problem after implementing the response. You use the same measures before and after the response. Clearly, you must plan the evaluation well in advance of the assessment.

Quantitative Measures

Quantitative measures involve numbers. The number of burglaries in an apartment complex is a quantitative measure. You can count such measures before and after the response, and note the difference. Quantitative measures allow you to use math to estimate the response's impact. For example, burglary rates drop 10 percent from before the response to after the response.

Qualitative Measures

Qualitative measures allow comparisons, but you cannot apply math to them. Though most evaluations use quantitative measures, qualitative measures can be extremely useful. Here is an example. Suppose you are trying to address a problem of gang-related violence in a neighborhood. From your analysis, you know that much of this violence stems from escalating turf disputes, and that graffiti is a useful indicator of intergang tension that can lead to violence.

You count the number of reported gunshots, gun injuries, and gun fatalities in the year before and the year after the response. These are quantitative measures. You also take monthly photos of known graffiti hot spots both before and after the response. By comparing the photos, you note that before the response, gang graffiti was quite common, and non-gang graffiti was rare. Further, many of the markings suggested that rival gangs were overwriting each other's graffiti. After the response, you find there is little gang graffiti, but non-gang graffiti has increased. Further, there is no evidence of overwriting in the little gang graffiti that you do find. This qualitative information reinforces the quantitative information by indicating that the response may have reduced gang tensions, or that the gangs have declined.

Maps can provide another qualitative measure. They are very useful for showing crime and disorder patterns. Though the number of crimes is a quantitative measure, the size and shape of the crime patterns are largely qualitative. You can use changes in these patterns to assess the effectiveness of responses.

Measurement Validity

You must make sure that quantitative and qualitative measures record the problem, and not something else. For example, counts of drug arrests are often better measures of police activity than of changes in a drug problem. You should use arrest data as a measure of the problem only if you are sure that police enforcement efforts and techniques have remained constant. Similarly, systematic covert surveillance of a drug-dealing hot spot before and after a response could be a valid measure if the surveillance has remained unchanged and undetected by drug dealers.

Measures are seldom definitively valid or invalid; rather, they are more or less valid than alternative measures. The more indirect the measure, the less valid. Surveillance entails direct observation. Arrest statistics are indirect. They involve the activities of the drug dealers and customers (the aspects of the problem you may be most interested in), but they also involve citizen decisions to bring the problem to police attention, and police decisions about whether (and how) to intervene. These citizen and police decisions may not always reflect the underlying reality of the problem. For example, changes in police overtime policies or the presence of special antidrug squads can change the number of arrests, even if the drug problem remains constant. For this reason, the number of drug dealer arrests is a less direct—and often poor—measure of a drug problem.

Here is another example of direct and indirect measures of a problem. In this example, what constitutes a direct measure and an indirect measure depends on how you define the problem. Suppose you are addressing a prostitution cruising problem. Men drive into a neighborhood on Friday and Saturday nights, looking for prostitutes to pick up. This annoys the residents, and they call the police. You have a choice of two measures for this problem.

The first is a quantitative measure taken from automatic traffic counters strategically placed on the critical streets three months before the response, and left there for three months after. These devices measure traffic flow. You use the difference between the average Friday and Saturday night traffic volume and the average volume during the rest of the week as an estimate of the traffic due to prostitution.

You base your second measure on interviews of residents conducted three months before and three months after the response. You ask residents to assess the prostitution problem, using a numerical scale (0 = none, 1 = minor, 2 = moderate, 3 = heavy).

If you have defined your problem as *prostitution-related traffic*, traffic volume is a more direct measure than residents' assessments. Not all of the difference between the Friday and Saturday traffic level and the level for the rest of the week is due to prostitution, but a large part of it probably is. So this is a reasonable approach to measuring the problem. Asking residents, however, is fraught with difficulties. Their current perceptions of prostitution may be colored by past observations. They may not see much of the prostitution traffic, particularly if they are staying indoors to avoid the problem. They may misperceive activities as prostitution-related, when they are not.

If, on the other hand, you have defined the problem as *residents' perceptions of prostitution-related traffic*, the interviews are a more direct measure than the traffic counts. Prostitution-related traffic may not have changed, but the residents think it has. By this measure, the response has been a success. But if prostitution-related traffic has declined precipitously, and the residents are unaware of it, then, by this measure, the response has not worked.

Of course, you can use multiple measures. In this example, you could measure both the prostitution-related traffic and the residents' perceptions of it. Only if both declined would you have an unambiguous success. If the traffic counters indicated a drop in traffic, but the interviews showed that the residents were unaware of it, then you could alter the response to address their perceptions.

In addition to taking the most direct measure of the problem possible, you also need to make sure you measure the problem systematically and follow the same measurement process throughout the entire evaluation. If, after the response, you photograph graffiti hot spots from different angles and distances than those used before, then it will be difficult to make valid comparisons. If the hot spots you photograph after the response are not the same ones you photographed before, then the validity of your comparison is highly questionable. This is because any difference noted might be due to how you collected the data, rather than to a real change in the problem.

In short, you want to make sure that any difference noted in the problem is due to changes in the problem, and not to changes in the way you measured it. One way of thinking about this is to compare it with physical evidence-gathering at a crime scene. The reason there are strict protocols for gathering and handling evidence is that we do not want to mistake the evidence gatherers' activities for those of the offender. The same holds true in evaluations.

Selecting Valid Measures

How do you select specific measures for your problem? There is no simple answer to this question that can be applied to any problem-solving effort. The guides in this series suggest measures for specific problems. If you are working on a problem not covered in a guide, then the simplest approach is to use one or more of the indicators you used to identify and analyze the problem. It is important, however, to think carefully about problem definition. As we saw in the prostitution example, seemingly minor changes in how we define the problem can have significant implications for measurement.

Clearly, you need to think about evaluation measures as soon as you begin the problem-solving process. If you wait until after you have implemented the response, then you might miss the chance to get valid "before" measures.

Criteria for Claiming Cause

There are two goals for a problem-solving assessment. The first is to determine if the problem has changed. We are particularly interested in whether it has declined. Only after establishing whether the problem has changed does the second goal—determining if the response *caused* the change—make sense.

If the problem has not changed, and if you do not intend to use a similar response to address other problems, then you don't need to worry about cause, and the evaluation is relatively simple. If, however, the problem has changed, and if you will likely use the response again, then it is important to determine if the response in fact caused the change. If the problem declined for reasons other than the response, then using the response to address similar problems is unlikely to reduce them. If the problem got worse for reasons other than the response, then the response might still be a useful way to address other problems. Consequently, it is important to understand what criteria we require to claim a response caused a change in a problem.

The concept of cause may seem pretty straightforward, but it is not. To be able to confidently proclaim that a response caused a problem to decline, you need to meet four criteria. The first three criteria are relatively straightforward and can often be met. The fourth criterion cannot be met with absolute certainty.

There Is a Plausible Explanation of How the Response Reduces the Problem†

The first criterion for claiming cause is that you have a plausible explanation of how the response reduces the problem. You should base this explanation on a detailed problem analysis, preferably augmented by prior research and theory. The fact that others used a similar response and reduced their problem is not an explanation. Such information is useful, but you still need to explain how the problem reduction occurred. Absent a convincing explanation, you do not know whether the response was successful by accident, whether the response was successful due to the particular situation in which it was first applied (and thus will not work on your problem), or whether the response is generally useful.

Here is an example to illustrate what is meant by a "plausible explanation." Suppose you have been working on a street prostitution problem, and you know that the prostitutes congregate along a three-block stretch of road (on B Street, between First and Fourth streets), one block off of a very busy thoroughfare (A Street). Each numbered street has traffic lights (see Figure 2 on page 20), and all of the streets are two-way. Between A and B streets are a largely vacant old warehouse and a light industrial area. The prostitutes and customers use this abandoned property. Customers enter B Street from A Street using the numbered streets, and circle the blocks looking for prostitutes.

---

† The technical term for this criterion is "mechanism." Wherever possible in this guide, commonly understood language has been substituted for the technical language of evaluators. Footnotes provide the technical terms for those interested in further study.

Figure 2. Street layout before and after a response to prostitution

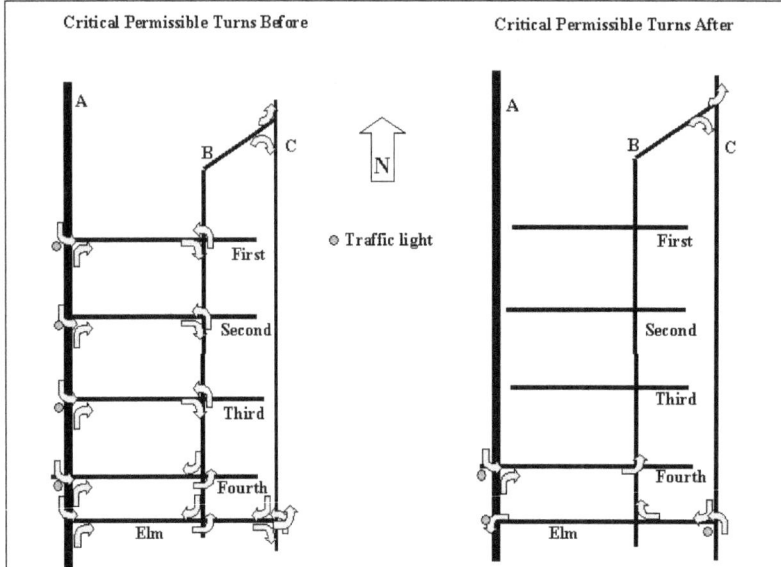

Between B and C streets is an old residential neighborhood of single-family homes called the Elms. C Street has become a thriving entertainment and arts area, and older Elms residents are selling their homes to younger, affluent couples. Residents complain about the traffic and noise, the harassing calls of the prostitutes and customers, and the litter (drink containers, condoms, and other debris).

To address this problem, residents propose a series of street changes. B Street will be made one-way north, and Elm Street one-way west, while Fourth Street will be made one-way east between A and B streets. The other numbered streets will be blocked off from A Street, and their traffic lights will be removed. A new traffic light will be placed at the intersection of Elm and A streets, but only left turns from Elm onto A will be permitted. Another traffic light will be placed at the intersection of Elm and C streets. The right side of Figure 2 shows these changes.

Why do the residents think this will work? We hope their explanation is plausible—that is, it is logical and takes into account the known facts. The residents claim the area is a hotbed of prostitution activity in large part because the streets facilitate solicitation. Customers can quickly cruise around the block looking for "dates." Changing the street patterns in the manner described will make circular cruising more time-consuming. If customers do not make a contact on the first pass, they will spend much more time on the return trip. By reducing the convenience of prostitution, fewer customers will come to the area, and the problem will decline. In addition, by streamlining the traffic flow, it will be easier for the police to detect prostitution-related activities. By observing customers and prostitutes, you can verify the cruising behavior. If this explanation is logically consistent with the available information, and if there is no obvious contradictory information, then the residents have leaped the first hurdle for establishing a causal connection.

A plausible explanation does not guarantee that the response will work; many plausible ideas do not work when tested. But it does make the response a more likely candidate for a successful solution. The explanation has added credibility in that previous research describes the relationship between prostitution and circular driving patterns,[3] and also indicates that reducing the ease of neighborhood traffic movement sometimes reduces crime.[4] Further, it is consistent with the theory of situational crime prevention, particularly the strategy of increasing offenders' effort.[5]

In summary, the first step in claiming cause is to have a plausible explanation of:

1. how the problem occurs, and

2. how the response reduces it.

This explanation should also cover when, where, and why the response works. If prepared at the time you are crafting the response, the explanation can help guide planning and implementation. The more specific the explanation, the better the response and the more informative the assessment. Ideally, the explanation will also describe the circumstances in which the response is unlikely to work. This can aid in both the process and the impact evaluations.

The Response and the Level of the Problem Are Related[†]

The second criterion for claiming cause is that there be a relationship between the presence of the response and a decline in the problem (and between the absence of the response and an increase in the problem).

---

† The technical term for this criterion is "association." Typically, association is measured by the correlation between the response and the level of the problem.

Let's go back to the prostitution problem. How would we demonstrate a relationship here? Just north of the Elms is a similar neighborhood (also between A and C streets, with a deteriorated light industrial area to the west, and the thriving C Street development to the east), but the streets do not allow for easy circular driving. Now if the ease of circular driving is associated with prostitution, then we should see little or no prostitution in this other neighborhood. This would imply that changing the Elms' street patterns might be helpful. However, if there is prostitution in this area, too, then there is not a strong link between prostitution and ease of circular driving, and this suggests that changing the street patterns may not be effective. Either way, the evidence would not be strong, but the findings could be helpful.

There is yet another way to examine a relationship. We might also measure the problem before and after the street changes. If we see high levels of prostitution-related traffic (or high levels of resident perceptions of it) before the changes, but low levels after the changes, we will have evidence of a relationship.

So the second hurdle to jump in claiming causation is to demonstrate that the problem is bigger in the absence of the response than when the response is in place. Though it is tempting to declare victory at this stage, we must surmount two other hurdles before we can be confident that the response caused the decline in the problem.

The Response Occurs Before the Problem Declines[†]

The third criterion for claiming cause simply requires that the response *precede* the decline in the problem. Since it is impossible for a response to have an effect before it is implemented, this criterion makes a lot of sense. There's one major caveat here: in defining "response," we include publicity *about* the response—intentional or accidental. A widespread media campaign may precede a drunken driving intervention, so that even before the intervention, potential drunken drivers may alter their behavior. In this case, the media campaign is part of the response. A decline in drunken driving *before* the media campaign would be evidence that something other than the response caused the decline. But a decline after the media campaign, but before the intervention, could be credited to the response.

Despite the obvious simplicity of this criterion, it is surprisingly common to see violations of it. Throughout the 1990s, homicides declined in large U.S. cities. In the middle of the decade, a few years into the downward trend, several cities implemented crime reduction strategies and gained substantial publicity. As homicides continued to decline in these cities, proponents claimed that the reductions were due to the new strategies. However, homicides

---

† The technical term for this criterion is "temporal order."

had been declining before the changes, so it is difficult to attribute the decline to them.[†] In short, the purported cause of the decline followed the decline. If, on the other hand, the cities had implemented the changes in 1990, the claim that the changes caused the drop in homicides would be more plausible.

To demonstrate that the response preceded the problem's decline, you must know when the response began (including publicity about it), and have measures of the problem before and after the response. This is a before-after (or pre-post) evaluation design. We saw this design in the prostitution example, when we described ways of demonstrating a relationship. We used a number of examples of pre-post designs in the section on measurement. Pre-post is the most common evaluation design, but it is not particularly strong; that is, a simple pre-post design can show a decline, but it is insufficient for establishing what caused it.

Despite its simplicity, this criterion can be difficult to meet. But even if you can show that the decline in the problem followed the response, you need to meet one more criterion before you can definitively claim that the response caused the decline.

There Are No Plausible Alternative Explanations[‡]

Let's continue with the prostitution problem. You have an explanation, you have demonstrated a relationship, and you have shown that the response preceded the decline in the problem. You now need to make sure that nothing else could have caused the decline. Recall that the C Street corridor and the Elms were going through a series of changes. New residents and the remaining older residents were trying to clean up the area. One thing they did was to ask the police to help. Did they do anything else? Suppose the Elms' Neighborhood Association (ENA) and the C Street Corridor Business Association (CSCBA) identified the owners of the abandoned and vacant property and put pressure on them to clean it up, denying prostitutes access to it. And suppose that this change occurred at about the same time the street changes did. So you could think of the ENA and the CSCBA as the cause of both the street *and* the land-use changes. If the land-use changes were the real cause of the decline in prostitution, and the street changes were irrelevant, you would still see a relationship between the street changes and the decline, and you would still see the response before the decline. Nevertheless, something else caused the decline.

---

† There is another reason to be skeptical that the changes in policing caused the decline in homicides. Homicides declined in other large cities that had not implemented the same changes. For a more detailed examination of the police contribution to the homicide decline in the 1990s, see Eck and Maguire (2000).

‡ The technical term for this criterion is "non-spuriousness." A spurious relationship is a hypothesized relationship between two or more variables that is false or misleading.

Figure 3 diagrams the notion of an alternative explanation. The upper half shows what you believe: the response caused the decline in the problem (as indicated by the arrow). This belief may come from a variety of valid sources. Nevertheless, something else caused the response, and something else caused the decline (lower half of the figure). Here, more "something else" led to more response and, at the same time, a reduction in the problem. The absence of an arrow between the response and the decline in the problem shows that the response was irrelevant to the decline. An outsider, observing more response and less of the problem, might conclude that the response caused the decline. In situations like this, the observed relationship between the response and the decline is misleading. The possibility of a misleading relationship is a threat to an evaluation's validity.

There is a related concern that should also be mentioned. The "something else" might not have prompted your problem-solving effort (as was the case in the prostitution example); rather, it might have occurred by coincidence at about the same time as your response. Practically speaking, it might not matter if the "something else" occurred at the same time as your response, or if the "something else" caused both the response and the decline. In neither case did the response cause the drop in the problem.

To demonstrate a causal connection between the response and the decline, you need to provide sound evidence that there is no "something else." To do so, you need to show that there are no reasonable explanations for the decline, other than the response. You do this by carefully examining the most obvious counterclaims and assessing evidence for them.

Figure 3. Alternative explanations

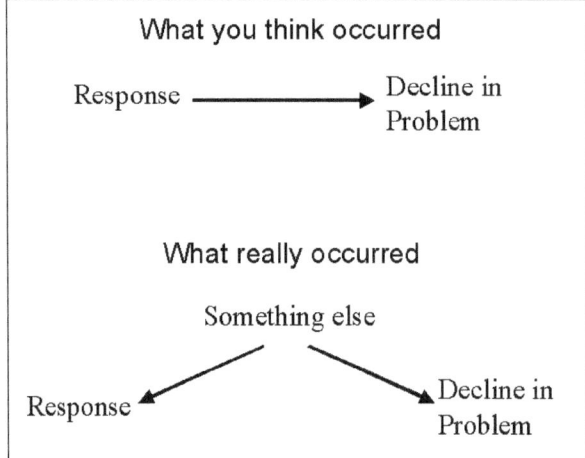

Ruling out alternative explanations is difficult. You can never do so definitively because there are many possible causes of problem fluctuations. All you can do is rule out the most obvious alternative explanations for the decline. In many respects, it is similar to demonstrating that a suspect committed a crime. The standards of evidence vary, depending on the decision being made. Stronger evidence is required to establish guilt in criminal court than to secure a warrant for an arrest. But in neither case is absolute evidence of guilt required. We can never prove that a response caused a decline in a problem because we cannot rule out all possible alternative explanations. We can make better or worse cases for such claims, however. And this is where the evaluation design comes in. Some designs allow for stronger statements of causality than others, just as some prosecutions are more plausible to a jury than others.

Evaluation Designs†

An evaluation design is a systematic strategy, coordinated with the response, for organizing when and where data collection will occur. If you develop the evaluation design along with the response, the evaluation is more likely to produce useful information. Waiting until after you have implemented the response to decide how you will evaluate it makes it more difficult to determine whether it was effective.

There are many types of evaluation designs (see the "Recommended Readings" section). We will discuss two common, practical designs: the pre-post and the interrupted time series. Appendix B describes designs using control groups: the pre-post with a control group, and the multiple time series. Table 2 summarizes the relationships among these four designs.

Table 2. Types of evaluation designs

	Single Measurement Before and After	Multiple Measurements Before and After
No Control Group	Pre-post	Interrupted time series
Control Group	Pre-post with a control group	Multiple time series

---

† Nonexperimental evaluation designs are not addressed in this guide because they often cannot demonstrate that the response preceded the decline in the problem, and because they are particularly poor at ruling out alternative explanations. Randomized evaluation designs are not addressed, either. Though powerful for studying generic interventions to apply to a class of problems, they are generally unsuited for operational problem-solving in which the primary interest is to reduce a specific problem. The publications listed under "Recommended Readings" provide information about these and other designs not described here.

Pre-Post Designs

The simplest pre-post design involves a single measurement of the problem both before and after the response. You then compare the measures. As we will see, this design is sometimes adequate for determining if the problem declined, but is insufficient for determining if the response caused the decline.[†]

Figure 4 illustrates the results of a pre-post design. The first bar shows the level of the problem before the response, and the second bar shows the level after. The difference between the heights of the bars represents the change in the problem. Though this example shows a decline, there is no guarantee; there could be an increase or no change in the problem (see Appendix A for an illustration).

Figure 4. Impact measurement in a pre-post design

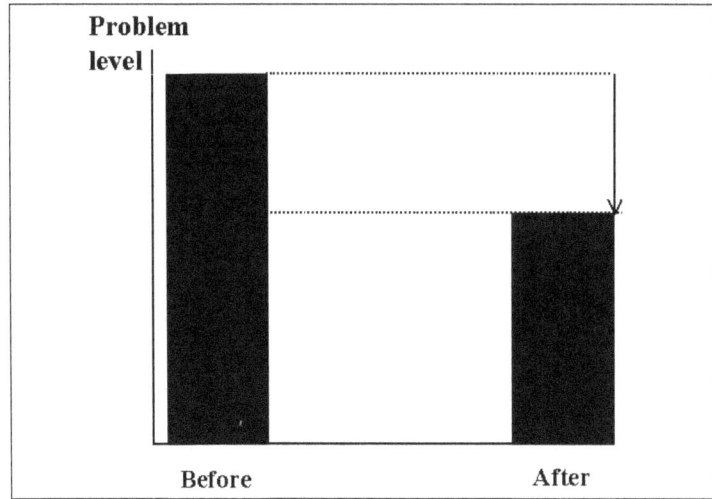

[†] In most evaluation research, a statistical significance test is used to determine if the difference between the pre- and post-response measures is likely due to chance. In other words, one alternative explanation is that normal random fluctuations in the problem level caused the difference between the before and after measures. A statistical significance test is most useful when the difference is small but nevertheless meaningful, and the number of problem events before the response was small. In such circumstances, normal random fluctuations are a potential cause for the change in the problem. Because of the highly technical nature of significance testing, this guide does not cover it. Readers interested in significance testing can learn more from most introductory statistics texts, the documentation accompanying statistical software, or statisticians and social scientists at local universities.

The pre-post design can establish a relationship by demonstrating that there was less of a problem with the response than without it. It also helps to demonstrate that the response preceded the decline, because the response occurred between the two measures. However, if the problem level normally fluctuates, then what you see as a decline may simply be a normal low before a return to a higher level. Variations on this simple design include taking measures at the same time of the year, to account for seasonal fluctuations, and taking two or three pre-measures and two or three post-measures, to account for other fluctuations.

As we have seen, this design is weak at ruling out alternative explanations for a decline in a problem. This is because something else may have caused the response and/or the decline. Consider two examples in which a pre-post design can give misleading results.

In the first example, suppose that, overall, the problem was declining, and this decline started before the pre-response measurement. If you knew this, then you would conclude that the decline would have occurred even if you had done nothing about the problem. Absent information about the downward trend, you would have false confidence in the response (Appendix A illustrates this in greater detail).

In the second example, the pre-post results show no change in the problem (or even a slight increase in it). Based on these results, you might believe the response was ineffective. However, if you knew that the long-term trend was for the problem to get much worse, then you might realize that the response might have averted much of that decline. In this case, the pre-post design gives the false impression that the response was ineffective.

When examining pre-post results, you should also consider when the response is implemented. Many problems fester for long periods, with many ups and downs. Even without any intervention, such problems fluctuate, though the fluctuations are around a constant average. Problem-solving efforts are more likely to be launched when problems are at their peak, and due to decline anyway. Thus, a decline may be due to this automatic process rather than to the response.[†] Next, we will examine designs that can rule out this particular alternative explanation.

---

† The technical term for this automatic process is "regression to the mean."

Interrupted Time Series Designs

The interrupted time series design is far superior to the pre-post design because it can address many of the issues discussed above. With this design, you take many measures of the problem before the response. This lets you look at the pre-response trend in the problem. You then take many measures of the problem after the response. Comparing the before trend with the after trend provides an indicator of effectiveness. This is feasible using reported crime data or other information routinely gathered by public and private organizations. It is more difficult if you have to initiate a special data collection effort, such as a public survey.

The basic approach is to use repeated measures of the problem before the response to forecast the likely problem level after the response. If the difference between the forecast and the measures taken after the response is significant and negative, this indicates that the response was effective (see Appendix A).

This design provides strong evidence that the response preceded the problem's decline, because you can identify preexisting trends. If the procedures for measuring the problem have not changed, this design rules out most alternative explanations for the decline, including the automatic-process explanation.

You should note that it is the number of measurement periods that matter, not the length of time. So, for example, annual data for the three years before and after the response are far less helpful than measurements for the 30 months before and after the response, even though less time has elapsed.

You might be tempted to take this to the extreme. If monthly data are better than annual data, why not collect weekly, daily or even hourly data? The answer is that, for most crimes, as the time interval becomes shorter, the number of crimes per interval becomes too small to derive meaningful conclusions. If the number of events is extremely large (as is sometimes the case when using calls-for-service data for large areas), then very short intervals might be useful. But if the number of events is very small (as with homicide or stranger-stranger rape), then you might have to use large intervals.

In Figure 5, the points on the graph represent measures of the problem taken at different times. The horizontal lines represent the trend (in this case, the average or mean) for the before and after periods. There is much variation around the mean values for both periods, and this variation can sometimes obscure response effects.

Figure 5. Impact measurement in an interrupted time series design

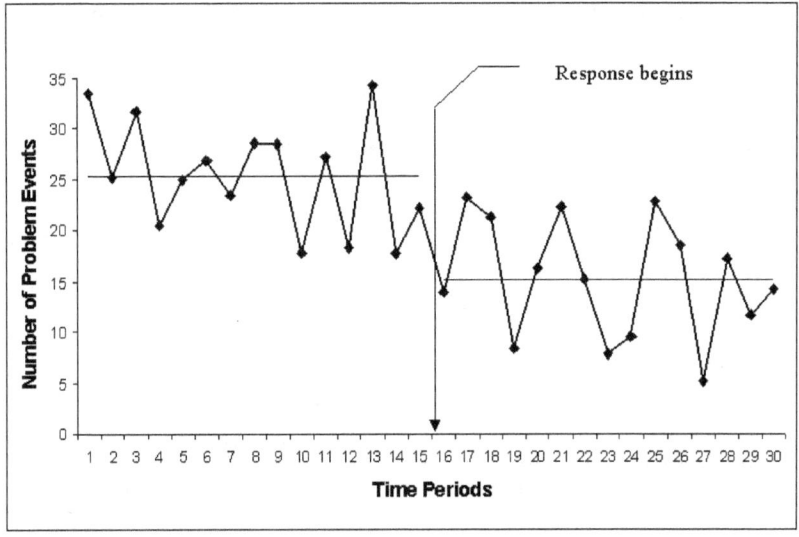

Since the trend is flat, the forecast is a horizontal-line projection based on the average number of incidents per time period. A comparison of the average problem level before and after the response shows a decline. If the problem had been trending up, then you would use an upward sloping projection and would have to calculate the slope (Appendix A provides an example). The more time periods you examine before the response, the more confident you can be that you know the problem's trajectory. The more time periods you examine after the response, the more confident you can be that the trajectory has changed. The calculations involved in analyzing an interrupted time series design can become quite involved, so if you have a lot riding on the evaluation's outcome, it may be worthwhile to seek expert help.

Ideally, the only difference between the time periods before and the time periods after the response is the presence of the response. If this is the case, then conclusions based on this design have a high degree of validity.

The major weakness of the interrupted time series design is the possibility that something else that occurred at the same time the response began caused the observed change in the problem. To rule out this alternative explanation, you can add a second time series for a control group (see Appendix B).

Even if you are interested in determining only whether the problem declined (and have little interest in establishing what caused the decline), an interrupted time series design is still superior to a pre-post design. This is because an interrupted time series design can show whether the problem went down and stayed down. As noted above, problems can fluctuate, so it is desirable to determine the decline's stability. The longer the time series after the decline, the greater your confidence that the problem has been eliminated or is stable at a much reduced level.

Though interrupted time series designs are superior to pre-post designs, they are not always practical. Here are five common reasons for this:
- Measurement is expensive or difficult.
- Data are unavailable for many periods before the response.
- Decision makers cannot wait for sufficient time to elapse after the response.
- Data recording practices have changed, making inter-period comparisons invalid.
- Problem events are rare for short time intervals, forcing you to use fewer, longer intervals.

Under these conditions, a pre-post design might be the most practical alternative.

Combining and Selecting Designs

Though we have examined pre-post and interrupted time series designs separately (here and in Appendix B), in many cases, you can use two or more designs to test a response's effectiveness. This is particularly useful if you have several measures of the problem (for example, reported crime data and citizen survey information) for different periods. Using a combination of designs selected to rule out particularly troublesome alternative explanations can be far more useful than strictly adhering to a single design.

In considering what type of design or combination of designs to use, you should bear in mind that you cannot rule out all alternative explanations for a problem's decline. Based on your available resources, you should select the simplest design that can rule out the most obvious alternative explanations. In other words, you should anticipate such explanations before you select the design. Once again, your analysis of the problem should give you some insight.

Before addressing spatial displacement of crime and disorder, and spatial diffusion of crime prevention benefits, we need to recall that there are two possible evaluation goals. The first is to demonstrate that the problem declined. The second is to have sufficient evidence to legitimately claim that the response caused the decline. The second goal is important only if you are going to use the response again. If so, you will need evidence that the response is effective—that it causes problems to decline. If you do not intend to use the response again (or to recommend it to others), then there is no real need to gather sufficient evidence to demonstrate that it caused the decline. In this case, you can say that there was a problem, you implemented a response, and the problem declined, but you do not know if the decline was due to the response or to other factors.

Spatial Displacement of Crime or Disorder, and Spatial Diffusion of Crime Prevention Benefits

A common concern about problem-solving responses is that they will result in spatial displacement of crime or disorder—the shifting of crime or disorder from the target area to nearby areas. This possibility is probably not as great as is imagined.[6] However, although displacement is far from inevitable, you should consider the possibility. In addition, there is increasing evidence that some responses have positive effects that spread beyond the target area. This is called spatial diffusion of crime prevention benefits. Though not all responses result in benefits beyond those planned for, some do, and you should also consider this possibility. If you do not account for displacement and diffusion, you could produce misleading evaluation results. To see how this can occur, and to learn how to address it, let's use a burglary problem as an example.

Suppose you have a 150-unit apartment complex that is beset by burglaries (we will call this the target complex). Across the street is a 120-unit complex that has some burglaries, but not as many as the target complex (we will call this the neighboring complex). Though built at different times, with somewhat different architectural designs, the complexes house occupants who are very similar with regard to income, race and number of children. Four miles away, there is a third, 180-unit complex that is also similar to the target complex. Now imagine that reported crime data show an average of 20 burglaries per month in the target complex before the response, and an average of 10 after the response (a 50 percent decline). Though this looks like a major success, you want to determine if the decline would have occurred regardless of the response.

Scenario A. You pick the neighboring complex as a control (see Appendix B), and you find that it had an average of seven burglaries per month before the response, and an average of 12 after the response. A control group is supposed to show what would have occurred absent a response, so you conclude—based on the increase in control group burglaries—that the target complex would also have experienced an increase, were it not for the response. Is this a valid conclusion? Maybe not. If displacement has occurred, about a quarter of the burglaries that *were* occurring in the target complex are *now* occurring in the neighboring complex. The response may have been successful, but not as successful as you thought. If crime or disorder shifts to a control area, then response success will be artificially inflated.

Scenario B. Burglaries in the neighboring complex drop from an average of seven a month before the response to an average of two after the response (a 71 percent decline). If the neighboring complex is the control group, then, on a percentage basis, the target complex did worse. Perhaps you would have been better off doing nothing.

But suppose that what really occurred was that the same burglars had been preying on both complexes. After the response, they decided to play it safe and reduced their efforts in both complexes. This means that instead of failing, the response was far more successful than anticipated. There was a diffusion of benefits from the target complex to the neighboring complex. Thus, using the neighboring complex as a control led you to vastly underestimate your response's success. If benefits extend to a control area, then response success will be artificially deflated.

Scenario C. You pick the complex four miles away as the control group, and use the neighboring complex to determine if displacement or diffusion occurred. If distance prevents the third complex from experiencing positive or negative effects, then it is a useful control group.

Figure 6 shows the relationship between a response area (R), a control area (C), and a displacement/diffusion area (D). C is not connected to the other areas, while D surrounds R. Such an arrangement is useful as long as the three areas are similar, and the control area is insulated from the response area, while the displacement/diffusion area is not.

Though distance can provide insulation, it is no guarantee. If R, C, and D are public housing complexes, and if the public housing authority moves tenants among them, then offenders in R will probably know about C, and may have acquaintances there. Consequently, C could be subject to displacement or diffusion. On the other hand, two areas may be close together, yet well insulated if there are major barriers to movement (e.g., rivers, canyons, or highways).

Figure 6. Handling possible spatial displacement and diffusion

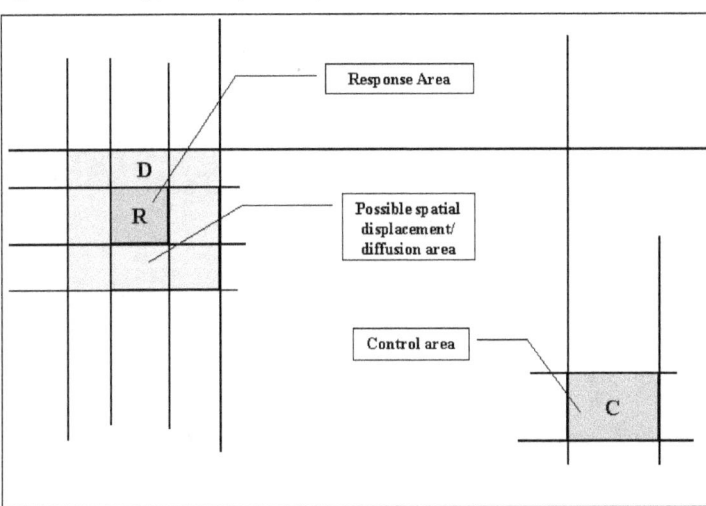

Comparing the target complex with the third complex gives you an estimate of the benefits of your response. Comparing the neighboring complex with the third complex tells you if displacement or diffusion occurred. You can combine the results to estimate the net effect (see Appendix C). If target-area burglaries dropped by 10, control-area burglaries dropped by three, and displacement/diffusion-area burglaries dropped by two, then the net reduction in burglaries per month would be –10 + 3 – 2 = –9. If displacement/diffusion-area burglaries increased by two, then the net reduction in burglaries per month would be –10 + 3 + 2 = –5. The basic principle is that you remove from the change in the problem the change that would have occurred anyway. You then increase the reduction in the problem if diffusion occurs, or decrease the reduction if displacement occurs.

Conclusions

This guide has introduced some basic principles of assessing the effectiveness of problem-solving efforts. All such evaluations require valid, systematic measures of the problem taken both before and after the response. There are two possible goals for any problem-solving evaluation. The first is to demonstrate that the problem declined enough to call an end to the response. This is the most basic requirement of an evaluation. In many circumstances, it is also useful to determine if the response caused the decline. If you anticipate using the response again on similar problems (or on the same problem, if it returns), then it is important to make this determination. This requires an evaluation that can rule out the most likely alternative explanations—one using either an interrupted time series design or a control group (see Appendix B). The control group tells you what the problem level would likely be, absent the problem-solving effort.

You should compare the results of the impact evaluation with those of the process evaluation to determine whether the response was implemented as planned, and what its impact was. With this information, you can adjust the response or craft a new one. This information should also aid others when they address similar problems.

A recurring theme in this guide is that the evaluation design builds on knowledge gained during the problem analysis. Competent evaluations require detailed knowledge of the problem so that you can develop useful measures and anticipate possible reasons for a decline in the problem following the response.

Evaluating prevention efforts can be extremely complex. For small-scale problem-solving efforts, in which the costs of mistaken conclusions are not serious, and weak causal inferences are tolerable, the information provided here should be sufficient. If, however, there is a lot riding on the outcome, it is important to show whether the response caused the drop in the problem, or there are serious consequences from drawing the wrong conclusions, then you should seek professional help in developing a rigorous evaluation. Once you have identified a problem, you should decide, as soon as possible, whether to enlist an outside evaluator's support to take adequate before measures and develop a rigorous design.

Appendix A: The Effects of the Number of Time Periods on the Validity of Evaluation Conclusions

To understand the importance of examining a large number of time periods, consider the following hypothetical example. All the charts that follow are from the same 40-period series (shown last in Figure A.4 on page 40). The response was implemented between periods 19 and 20. Figures A.1 through A.3 show what an evaluator would see if they selected different time periods on either side of the implementation. As you will see, these different views suggest different conclusions.

Figure A.1. Two-period pre-post design

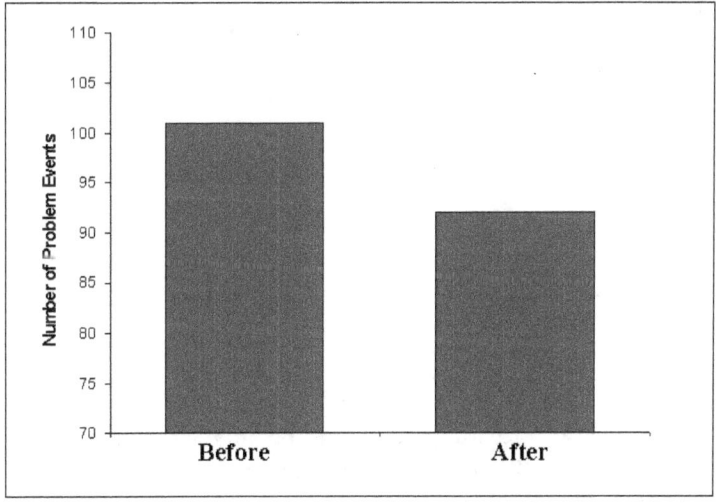

Figure A.2 shows nine time periods—12 through 20 in the series—eight periods before the response, and one after the response. Using more periods provides an opportunity to examine the trend in the problem before the response. The straight line shows this trend (trajectory). Extending the trajectory to one period beyond when response begins allows us to compare what we might expect if the response were not implemented (the trajectory) with the actual problem level.

Figure A.2. Nine-period time series design

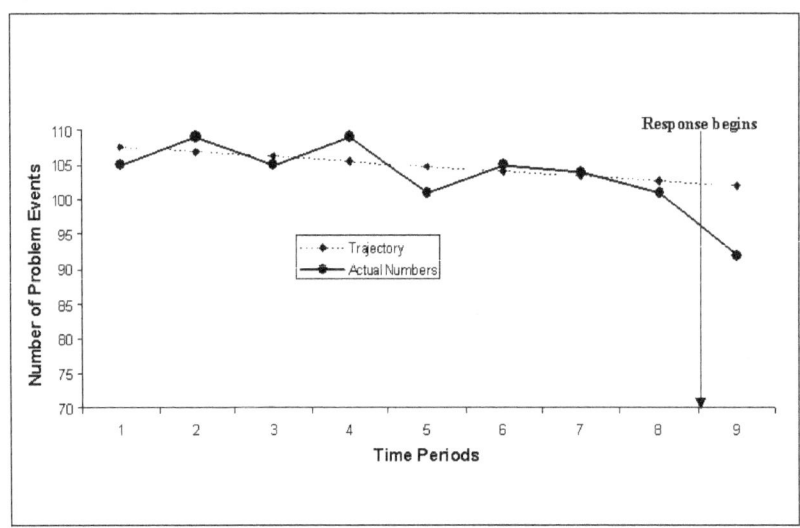

We can plainly see that the problem was trending downward before the response—that is, the response did not cause the entire decline. Nevertheless, it appears that there was a greater drop in the problem after the response than we would have expected due to the trend alone.

The periods before the response help establish the trajectory of the problem time series. Here we focused exclusively on the overall trend, but it is also possible to look for seasonal and other recurring fluctuations.

Extending the data to several periods after the response helps us determine the response's stability. Does the response continue to be effective, further reducing the problem? Or does the response wear off, allowing the problem to rebound? Figure A.3 shows an additional seven periods after the response. Based on the pre-response data, the same trend line is used, but it is now projected out eight periods after the response. We see that the problem rebounded and then seemed to oscillate around the trend line. So at best, the response was temporarily helpful.

Figure A.3. 16-period time series design

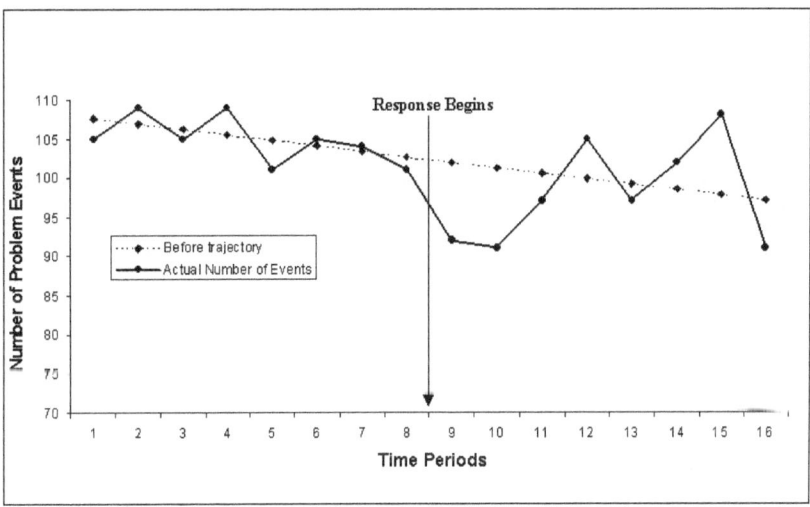

It would be tempting to end the story here, but it is worth examining the entire 40-period series from which the three previous figures were extracted. Figure A.4 shows this series.

It turns out that this time series has a flat trajectory. The problem level oscillates around 100 events per period. Further undermining our confidence in the response, we see that there are at least two pre-response periods with declines like those we see after the response. So it appears that what we thought was a decline due to the response may very well be a temporary fluctuation due to normal variations in the problem.

Figure A.4. 40-period time series design

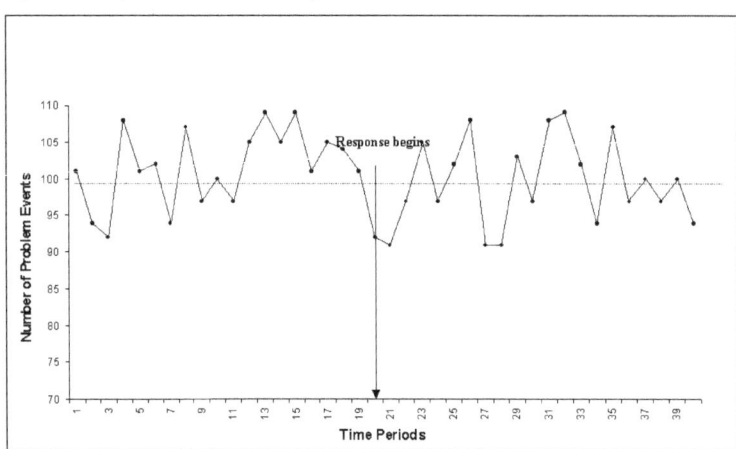

Unlike real data—with which we are never quite sure of the cause—with this artificial data, we know with absolute certainty that the variations around the 100 events per period are random.[†] This includes the periods just before and after the response. The example shows that we can easily misinterpret random data fluctuations as meaningful changes. It is worth noting that a significance test to detect randomness in a pre-post design might actually suggest that a drop is not due to random changes. This is because randomness affects the entire series, and the pre-post design covers only a small part of the series.

---

† That is because this data series was created by setting a constant level for the problem, and then using a random number generator to provide the fluctuations around that level.

Appendix B: Evaluation Designs With Control Groups

The evaluation designs discussed in the body of the text focus on data for the area receiving the response. If you want to determine whether the response caused the drop in the problem, it is often helpful to use a control group. Also, control groups are critical to obtaining reasonable estimates of the amount of spatial displacement and diffusion. You can use control groups with both the pre-post and the interrupted time series designs.

Pre-Post Design With a Control Group†

An improvement on the pre-post design is the addition of a control group. The control group does not receive the response, even though it has a problem similar to the response group's. As noted above, *the purpose of the control group is to demonstrate what would have occurred, absent the response.* Knowing this can help you rule out some alternative explanations for the decline in the problem.

For example, say you are concerned that a burglary decline in an apartment complex where you implemented a response may simply reflect an overall, citywide decline in residential burglary. To rule out this alternative explanation, you measure burglaries in apartment complexes similar to the one receiving the response. If the target complex had a greater reduction than the control group, you can rule out the citywide trend as a possible cause of the decline. Your confidence in your findings is directly proportional to the similarity between the response and control groups.

Figure B.1 on page 42 shows an example of a pre-post design with a control group. It indicates that the response was ineffective, because the control group's problem declined more than the response group's. In other words, the control group's decline suggests that, absent a response, the problem would have declined more than it did with the response. In this example, the response made things worse.

---

† This design is usually referred to as a "nonequivalent control group design" to draw attention to the fact that members of the response group and members of the control group may be different in ways that could affect the evaluation results.

Figure B.1. Impact measurement in a pre-post design with a control group

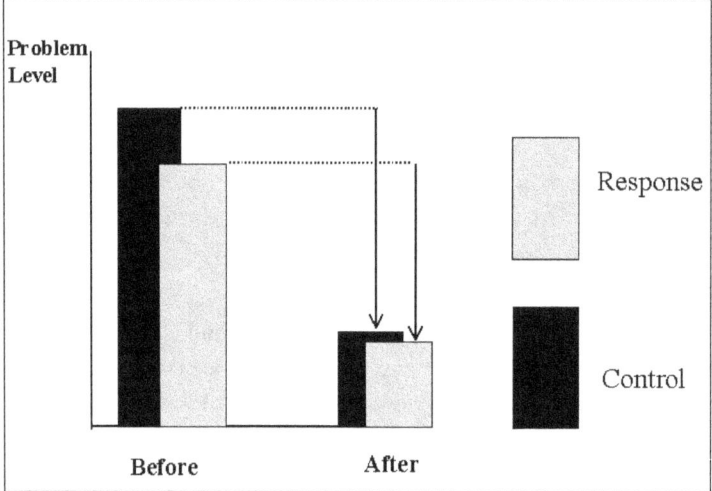

A potential weakness of the pre-post design with a control group is the possibility that the differences between the response and control groups, and not the response, caused the change in the problem. In other words, the control group does not provide a valid measure of what would have happened in the response group, absent the response. For example, say you want to evaluate a response to thefts from autos parked at a shopping mall. Instead of using another mall, with a similar problem, as the control, you use the downtown central business district (CBD). Though the mall and CBD may have superficially similar problems, the parking patterns (lots vs. streets), shopping patterns (evenings and weekends vs. weekdays), street patterns (suburban vs. urban), etc., might make the CBD too different from the mall for it to be a valid control group. A better control group would be one that shares many characteristics that could contribute to thefts from autos (similar parking lots with similar security, similar shopping patterns, etc.).

A control group should share as many characteristics as possible with the response group. Ideally, they would be the same, but this is usually impossible in operational settings. Since control and response groups will be similar in some ways but not in others, in which ways should they be most similar? Obviously, the answer depends on the problem being addressed. The best control group is one that has the same type of problem and in which the response would be a plausible intervention. In other words, the explanation for how the response works (the first criterion needed to establish causality) would apply equally well to both groups.

Even under these conditions, this design may not rule out some alternative explanations. Consider the concern that automatic processes cause a decline. If the response group has an abnormally high problem level, and the control group has an abnormally low problem level, then the response group will automatically improve, and the control group will automatically get worse, regardless of the response. To rule out this alternative explanation, you need evidence that the response group did not have an abnormally high problem level, and that the control group did not have an abnormally low problem level. Another way to rule out this alternative explanation is to use a time series design. In the body of the text, we examined a simple time series. You can improve this design by adding a control time series.

Multiple Time Series Design

When you use two or more time series, you are using a multiple time series design. This design can rule out most alternative explanations for a change in a problem. Figure B.2 illustrates a multiple time series. The fluctuating solid line represents the problem levels for the response group before and after the response. The flat solid lines represent the average pre- and post-response problem levels for that group. Though difficult to see, there is a definite decline in the average problem level after the response.

The dashed lines represent the trends for the control group. The problem has slightly worsened for this group after the response. This suggests that, absent a response, the problem would not have changed, and may have gotten worse.

Figure B.2. Impact measurement in a multiple time series design

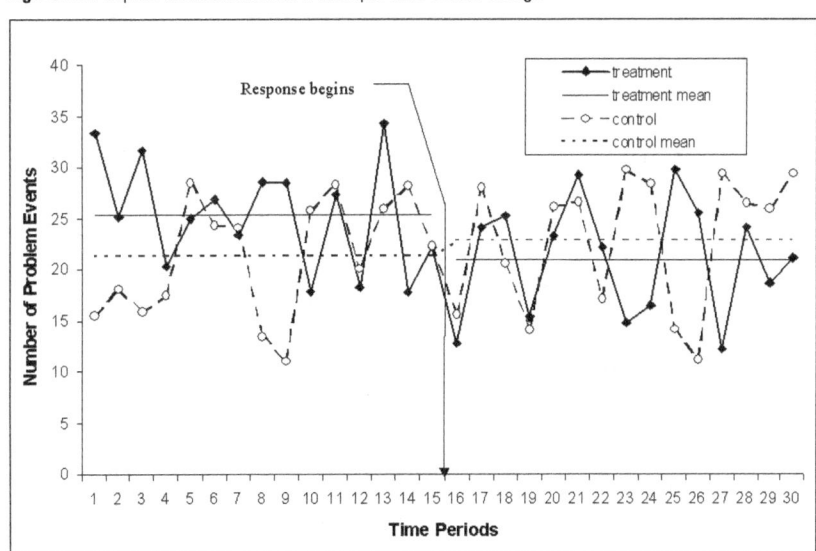

Appendix C: Calculating a Response's Net Effect

What is a response's net effect, taking into account changes in the problem that would have occurred anyway (as shown in the control area), and displacement or diffusion (as shown in a nearby, similar area)? For each of the three areas—response, control, and displacement/ diffusion—you take pre- and post-response measures that might show an increase or a decrease in their problem levels.

Because the three areas can have different base levels of crime, you must standardize the changes in crime from before to after the response. To do so, for each area, you divide the difference in crime by the amount of crime in the before period. The result is a proportional change in crime. The formula is as follows: (crime after − crime before)/(crime before) = proportional change in crime.

The net effect is the sum of the three proportional changes. But because we are dealing with crime and other harmful activities, we are interested in declines. We treat a decline in the problem in the response area as a negative number (since the before number is greater than the after number). Similarly, we treat a decline in the displacement/diffusion area as a negative number. (A decline in that area indicates diffusion, whereas an increase indicates displacement.) We treat a decline in the control area as a positive number, and an increase as a negative number. This ensures that if the control and response areas' problem levels change in the same direction by the same amount, the net effect will be zero (assuming no displacement or diffusion).

Table C.1 shows the sign (positive or negative) to use for each area, depending on the direction of change from before to after. Totaling these changes, using the appropriate sign, provides the response's net effect. Note that if the response area has an increase, the control area has an even greater increase, and there is no displacement or diffusion, then the net effect is negative, suggesting that the response kept the problem level lower than it would have been otherwise.

Table C.1. Signs used for calculating a response's net effect

	Change in Problem Level	
	Decline	Increase
Response Area	—	+
Displacement/Diffusion Area	—	+
Control Area	+	—

Appendix D: Summary of Evaluation Designs' Strengths and Weaknesses

Design	Strengths	Weaknesses
Pre-Post	• Is simple and quick to implement • Can easily be used with surveys • Can provide a reasonable estimate of the post-response change in the problem	• Can show only short-term changes in the problem • Cannot account for preexisting trends • Cannot account for the possibility that some other factor occurred at the same time as the response, and caused the problem to change • Is very weak at ruling out other alternative explanations
Interrupted Time Series	• Is easy to use with data routinely collected over many time periods • Can rule out preexisting trends and many other alternative explanations	• Is very hard to use if special data collection methods, such as surveys, are used to measure the problem • Cannot account for the possibility that some other factor occurred at the same time as the response, and caused the problem to change • Takes a long time to establish results • Is hard to interpret when there are few problem events per time period before the response
Pre-Post With a Control Group	• Can easily be used with surveys • Can account for the possibility that some other factor occurred at the same time as the response, and caused the problem to change	• Can show only short-term changes in the problem • Requires a control group that is similar to the response group
Multiple Time Series	• Is easy to use with data routinely collected over many time periods • Can rule out preexisting trends and many other alternative explanations • Can account for the possibility that some other factor occurred at the same time as the response, and caused the problem to change	• Is very hard to use if special data collection methods, such as surveys, are used to measure the problem • Requires a control group that is similar to the response group • Takes a long time to establish results • Is hard to interpret when there are few problem events per time period before the response

Appendix E: Problem-Solving Evaluation Checklist

The following checklist provides a summary of the issues you should consider in evaluating a problem-solving effort. It should be interpreted as a general guide, and not as a set of rigid rules. This checklist is most helpful if used throughout the problem-solving process, beginning in the scanning stage.

I. Early Considerations

You should consider the following questions during the scanning, analysis and response stages.

A. What will the evaluation help you decide?

❏ 1. Should you continue the problem-solving effort? If this is the *only* decision the evaluation will help you make, then a simple evaluation design will be sufficient (see question III.A).

❏ 2. Should either your agency or other agencies use the response for similar problems? If so, then you should consider using a control group in the evaluation design (see question III.A).

❏ 3. There is no decision to make. If no decision is required, then an evaluation will not be helpful.

B. Do you know the problem? (You need to answer these questions with some precision to develop and evaluate a cost-effective response. If you cannot answer them with some precision, then you should do more to analyze the problem.)

❏ 1. Whom does the problem harm? Whom does it not harm?

❏ 2. How can you measure the harm?

❏ 3. Where does the problem occur? Where does it not occur?

❏ 4. When does the problem occur? When does it not occur?

❏ 5. What causes the problem? What prevents or reduces it?

C. Do you know how the response works? (You need to answer these questions to determine if the response is likely to be effective, and to ensure accountability during implementation. If you cannot answer them, then your response plans are inadequate, and you need to focus more on the response stage.)

☐ 1. How does the response affect the causes
   of the problem?
☐ 2. Who is responsible for implementing the response?
☐ 3. When is the response supposed to be implemented?
☐ 4. Where is the response supposed to be implemented?
☐ 5. How long does the response take to have a noticeable
   effect on the problem?
☐ 6. Who has the legal authority to implement the response?
☐ 7. What are the likely barriers to implementing
   the response?

II. Process Evaluation

The process evaluation begins toward the end of the response stage, and continues well into the assessment stage.

A. Did you implement the response? (The closer the actual implementation is to the planned response, the greater confidence you have that the response caused the problem change documented in the impact evaluation. The more variation between what you intended and what occurred, the greater the likelihood that factors other than the response caused changes in the problem.)

☐ 1. Did you implement the response when you were
   supposed to?
☐ 2. Did you implement the response where you were
   supposed to?
☐ 3. Did you implement the response for the
   appropriate group?
☐ 4. Did you otherwise implement the response as planned?

B. Did you implement enough of the response? (You may have implemented the response, but without the resources, duration, or intensity needed to make it effective.)

❑ 1. Did you have sufficient resources to fully implement the response?

❑ 2. Did you implement the response long enough to have an effect?

❑ 3. Did you implement the response with sufficient intensity?

III. Impact Evaluation

Many of the decisions you need to make to conduct an impact evaluation should be considered in the analysis and response stages. This is particularly true of measurement decisions.

A. Do you need a control group? (Answering these questions helps you decide on the complexity of the evaluation design.)

❑ 1. Did you check question I.A.1? If so, then you do not need a control group.

❑ 2. Did you check question I.A.2? If so, then you should use a control group.

B. How often can you measure the problem? (Answering these questions helps you to decide whether a time series design is possible.)

❑ 1. Can you measure the problem consistently for many time periods before and after the response? If so, then a time series design is feasible.

❑ 2. Can you measure the problem only a few times before and after the response? If so, then a time series design is not feasible, and you need to use a pre-post design.

❑ 3. Can you take some measures of the problem for many time periods before and after the response, and other measures for only a few time periods before and after the response? If so, then you can use both a time series and a pre-post design.

C. What type of evaluation design should you use? (Your answers to the questions in sections A and B, immediately above, provide some basic guidance for answering this question, as shown in Table E.1. Obviously, precise answers depend on the particular circumstances of each problem-solving effort.)

Table E.1. Which evaluation design makes the most sense?

B. Question Checked	A. Question Checked	
	1	2
1	Interrupted time series design	Multiple time series design
2	Pre-post design	Pre-post design with a control group
3	Combination of designs above	Combination of designs above

D. What type of control group do you need? (This question applies only if you chose one of the options from column 2 under "A. Question Checked" above. If you chose an option from column 1, then skip this section and go to part IV.)

❏ 1. Will you apply the response to an identifiable geographic area (place, neighborhood, etc.)? If so, then the control group should be a very similar geographic area—with a similar problem—preferably located some distance from the response area.

❏ 2. Will you apply the response to a group of identifiable potential victims (young males, elderly women, commuters, etc.)? If so, then the control group should be a very similar group of potential victims.

❏ 3. Will you apply the response to a group of identifiable potential offenders? If so, then the control group should be a very similar group of potential offenders.

❏ 4. Will you apply the response to some other identifiable group of people or things? If so, then the control group should be a very similar group of people or things.

❏ 5. Are you unable to identify a control group for this evaluation? If so, then go back to Table E.1 and pick the appropriate option from column 1 under "A. Question Checked." Then go to part IV.

If you checked one of the first four questions above, then systematically compare the response group's characteristics with the control group's characteristics, and list the major differences. In part V, you will consider whether other factors might have caused the change in the problem. Your list of differences is a list of potential "other factors."

IV. Evaluation Conclusions

The following questions fall within the assessment stage and are applicable once you have documented your evaluation results. These questions are designed to help you draw conclusions consistent with your process and impact evaluation results and your evaluation design. You will have to ask more questions than listed here to fully interpret your particular evaluation results.

A. What are your findings from the process evaluation?

- ❑ 1. You did not implement the response.
- ❑ 2. You implemented the response in a radically different manner than planned.
- ❑ 3. You implemented the response with insufficient resources, for too short a time, or without the required intensity.
- ❑ 4. You implemented the response almost as planned, and with sufficient resources, for the necessary time, and with the required intensity.

B. What are your findings from the impact evaluation? (Select the design you used—pre-post, pre-post with a control group, time series, or multiple time series. If you used a combination of designs, then interpret your evaluation for each design separately, using tables E.2 and E.3.)

Pre-post design: Use Table E.2 to interpret your evaluation.

- ❑ 1. The problem got worse after the response.
- ❑ 2. The problem did not change after the response.
- ❑ 3. The problem declined after the response.

Pre-post design with a control group: Use Table E.3 to interpret your evaluation.

❑ 1. The response group's problem got worse, relative to the
control group's.
❑ 2. The response group's problem did not change, relative
to the control group's.
❑ 3. The response group's problem declined, relative to the
control group's.

Time series design: Use Table E.3 to interpret your evaluation.

❑ 1. The problem got worse after the response.
❑ 2. The problem did not change after the response.
❑ 3. The problem declined after the response.

Multiple time series design: Use Table E.3 to interpret your evaluation.

❑ 1. The response group's problem got worse, relative to the
control group's.
❑ 2. The response group's problem did not change, relative
to the control group's.
❑ 3. The response group's problem declined, relative to the control group's.

V. Overall Impact Evaluation Conclusions

The answers to the following questions are judgment calls and reflect your degree of
confidence in the findings, rather than a totally objective assessment of what occurred.
Other people, examining the same evidence, could come to different conclusions. For this
reason, you should answer these questions (and the question that follows) after several
people with different perspectives have examined the assessment information.

❑ 1. Did the problem decline after the response?

❑ 2. If the problem did decline, did it do so at a faster rate after the response than before the response?

❑ 3. If the problem did decline, can you rule out all other plausible explanations for the decline, other than the response? Use your list of differences between the response and control groups to help answer this question.

Based on your answers to the preceding questions, **are you reasonably confident that the response caused the decline (if any) in the problem**?

Table E.2. Interpreting results of process and impact evaluations (pre-post designs)

		Process Evaluation Results Answers to Question IV.A	
		4 checked: You implemented the response almost as planned.	**1, 2, or 3 checked:** You did not implement the response; implemented it in a radically different manner than planned; or implemented it with insufficient resources, for too short a time, or without the required intensity.
Impact Evaluation Results Answers to Question IV.B *(pre-post design)*	**3 checked:** The problem declined.	**A.** The response may or may not have caused the decline in the problem. Nevertheless, the decline occurred.	**C.** This suggests that other factors may have caused the decline in the problem, or the response was accidentally effective. Nevertheless, the decline occurred.
	1 or 2 checked: The problem got worse or did not change.	**B.** The response does not seem to have worked, though it is possible the problem would have increased (or increased even more) without it.	**D.** You have learned little from this evaluation. It is unclear whether you should implement the planned response, or reanalyze the problem and try a different response.
Regardless of the interpretation (A, B, C, or D), you have insufficient evidence to link the response to the problem level. The impact evaluation results neither support nor rule out using the response for similar problems.			

❏ 1. **Yes**–If you have thoroughly considered the questions and have answered "Yes" to all of them, then Table E.3 may be helpful. If you used only a pre-post design, then you cannot answer "Yes" to questions 2 and 3. If you used only a pre-post design with a control group, then you cannot answer "Yes" to question 2.

❏ 2. **No**–If you answered "No" to *any* of the three questions, then you must interpret Table E.3 with extreme caution. Any recommendations you make regarding the response should entail a frank discussion of alternative explanations.

Table E.3. Interpreting results of process and impact evaluations (other designs)

		Process Evaluation Results Answers to Question IV.A	
		4 checked: You implemented the response almost as planned.	**1, 2, or 3 checked:** You did not implement the response; implemented it in a radically different manner than planned; or implemented it with insufficient resources, for too short a time, or without the required intensity.
Impact Evaluation Results Answers to Question IV.B *(pre-post design with a control group, time series design or multiple time series design)*	**3 checked:** The problem declined.	**A.** This is evidence that the response caused the decline in the problem. The response is a potentially useful option for similar problems.	**C.** This suggests that other factors may have caused the decline in the problem, or the response was accidentally effective. You should not recommend this response to address similar problems, since you do not know if it would have an impact.
	1 or 2 checked: The problem got worse or did not change.	**B.** This is evidence that the response was ineffective. The response probably should not be used for similar problems. You should reanalyze the problem and try a different response.	**D.** You have learned little from this evaluation. Perhaps if you had implemented the response as planned, you would have had better results, but this is speculative. No recommendations—either for or against the response—are valid.

Endnotes

1. Pawson and Tilley (1997).

2. Eck and Spelman (1987); Office of Community Oriented Policing Services (1998).

3. Matthews (1992).

4. Eck (2002).

5. Clarke (1992).

6. Cornish and Clarke (1986); Eck (1993); Hesseling (1995).

7. Clarke and Weisburd (1994).

References

Clarke, R. (1992). *Situational Crime Prevention: Successful Case Studies*. Albany, NY: Harrow and Heston.

Clarke, R., and D. Weisburd (1994). "Diffusion of Crime Control Benefits: Observations on the Reverse of Displacement." In R. Clarke (ed.), *Crime Prevention Studies*, Vol. 2. Monsey, NY: Criminal Justice Press.

Cornish, D., and R. Clarke (1986). "Situational Prevention, Displacement of Crime and Rational Choice Theory." In K. Heal and G. Laycock (eds.), *Situational Crime Prevention: From Theory Into Practice*. London: Her Majesty's Stationery Office.

Eck, J. (2002). "Preventing Crime at Places." In L. W. Sherman, D. Farrington, and B. Welsh (eds.), *Evidence-Based Crime Prevention*. New York: Routledge.

———— (1993). "The Threat of Crime Displacement." *Criminal Justice Abstracts* 25:527–546.

Eck, J., and E. Maguire (2000). "Have Changes in Policing Reduced Violent Crime? An Assessment of the Evidence." In A. Blumstein and J. Wallman (eds.), *The Crime Drop in America*. New York: Cambridge University Press.

Eck, J., and W. Spelman (1987). *Problem-Solving: Problem-Oriented Policing in Newport News*. Washington, D.C.: Police Executive Research Forum.

Hesseling, R. (1995). "Displacement: A Review of the Empirical Literature." In R. Clarke (ed.), *Crime Prevention Studies*, Vol. 3. Monsey, NY: Criminal Justice Press.

Matthews, R. (1992). "Developing More Effective Strategies for Curbing Prostitution." In R. Clarke (ed.), *Situational Crime Prevention: Successful Case Studies* (1st ed.). New York: Harrow and Heston.

Office of Community Oriented Policing Services (1998). *Problem-Solving Tips: A Guide to Reducing Crime and Disorder Through Problem-Solving Partnerships*. Washington, D.C.: U.S. Department of Justice, Office of Community Oriented Policing Services.

Pawson, R., and N. Tilley (1997). *Realistic Evaluation*. London: Sage.

About the Author

John E. Eck

John Eck is Professor of Criminal Justice at the University of Cincinnati, where he teaches graduate courses in research methods, police effectiveness, crime policy, and crime prevention. With Ronald V. Clarke, he is the coauthor of *Becoming a Problem-Solving Crime Analyst*. Eck received his doctorate from the University of Maryland in 1994, and a master's degree in public policy from the University of Michigan in 1977. From 1977 to 1994, he directed research at the Police Executive Research Forum, in Washington, D.C., where he conducted studies of criminal investigations management and drug markets, and helped to test and implement problem-oriented policing in agencies throughout the United States. From 1995 to 1998, Eck was the evaluation coordinator for the Washington/Baltimore High-Intensity Drug Trafficking Area, where he developed methods for assessing the effectiveness of drug trafficking enforcement. Eck has written extensively on problem-oriented policing, crime mapping, drug markets, computer simulation of crime patterns, and crime prevention. He was a member of the National Academy of Sciences Committee on Police Policy and Research and is a judge for the British Home Office's Tilley Award for Problem-Solving Excellence. Eck's research interests include the causes and prevention of crime and disorder, and the ways crime patterns develop and change.

Recommended Readings

The following publications provide more extensive information about evaluation methods. Some were written for police, others for undergraduate students, and still others for research practitioners.

Bachman, Ronet, and Russell K. Schutt (2001). *The Practice of Research in Criminology and Criminal Justice.* Thousand Oaks, California: Pine Forge Press.

This college-level text provides a well-written description of the theory and practice of data collection, measurement and research design as applied to criminal justice research and evaluation.

Campbell, Donald T., and Julian C. Stanley (1963). *Experimental and Quasi-Experimental Designs for Research.* New York: Houghton Mifflin.

This is the "bible" of evaluation designs. Virtually every methods text adapts material from this book. It is still indispensable, and though short and to the point, it is not a fast read.

Clarke, Ronald V. (1992). *Situational Crime Prevention: Successful Case Studies.* Albany, New York: Harrow and Heston.

The case studies in this volume illustrate a wide variety of evaluation design applications.

Converse, Jean M., and Stanley Presser (1986). *Survey Questions: Handcrafting the Standardized Questionnaire.* Thousand Oaks, California: Sage.

This book is a standard reference in survey research. Its title explains its content.

Czaja, Ronald, and Johnny Blair (1996). Designing Surveys: *A Guide to Decisions and Procedures.* Thousand Oaks, California: Pine Forge Press.

This is a good introductory guide to survey question design.

Eck, John E., and Nancy La Vigne (1994). *Using Research: A Primer for Law Enforcement Managers* (2nd ed.). Washington, D.C.: Police Executive Research Forum.

This short book was developed for practicing police officials who have no background in research or statistics. It addresses most of the fundamentals and serves as a bridge to more-advanced introductory texts used in most college courses.

Eck, John E., and Nancy La Vigne (1993). *Police Guide to Surveying Citizens and Their Environment.* Washington, D.C.: Bureau of Justice Assistance. NCJ No. 143711.

This monograph describes the basics of conducting surveys of the public and of the physical environment. It contains a number of examples and survey instruments. It can be downloaded from www.ncjrs.org.

Harries, Keith (1999). *Mapping Crime: Principle and Practice*. Washington, D.C.: National Institute of Justice, U.S. Department of Justice.

This is an excellent introduction to the principles of crime mapping.

Hoover, Larry T. (1998). *Police Program Evaluation*. Washington, D.C.: Police Executive Research Forum and Sam Houston State University.

This compendium of articles describes how evaluation can be applied to a variety of police functions. Though not tailored explicitly for problem-oriented projects, the examples and concepts are often transferable.

Kosslyn, Stephen M. (1994). *Elements of Graph Design*. New York: W.H. Freeman.

This well-organized book offers practical and straightforward advice on how to create effective charts, graphs and figures with data. It is filled with good and bad examples.

Trochim, William, and James P. Donnelly (2007). *The Research Methods Knowledge Base*. 3rd ed. Cincinnati, Ohio: Atomicdog. www.atomicdogpublishing.com

This college text was designed for use online, but is available in a paperback version. It is very practical and shows how to create complex evaluation designs out of simpler designs in order to address particular situations. It also contains an excellent discussion of measurement and sampling.

Weisburd, David (1998). *Statistics in Criminal Justice*. Belmont, California: Wadsworth.

This is a very well-written introductory college text in statistics, taking the reader from the very basics to an intermediate level.

Weisel, Deborah (1999). *Conducting Community Surveys: A Practical Guide for Law Enforcement Agencies*. Washington, D.C.: Bureau of Justice Statistics and Office of Community Oriented Policing Services. NCJ No. 178246.

This practical guide for law enforcement agencies accompanies the crime victimization survey software developed by the Bureau of Justice Statistics and the Office of Community Oriented Policing Services. It describes how surveys have been used to improve policing services, how to identify survey goals, and the procedures for survey administration and analysis. It can be downloaded from www.puborder.ncjrs.org.

Other Problem-Oriented Guides for Police

Problem-Specific Guides Series

1. **Assaults in and Around Bars, 2nd Edition.** Michael S. Scott and Kelly Dedel. 2006. ISBN: 978-1-935676-64-5
2. **Street Prostitution, 2nd Edition.** Michael S. Scott and Kelly Dedel. 2006. ISBN: 1-932582-01-0
3. **Speeding in Residential Areas, 2nd Edition.** Michael S. Scott with David K. Maddox. 2010. ISBN: 978-1-935676-02-7
4. **Drug Dealing in Privately Owned Apartment Complexes.** Rana Sampson. 2001. ISBN: 1-932582-03-7
5. **False Burglar Alarms, 2nd Edition.** Rana Sampson. 2007. ISBN: 1-932582-04-5
6. **Disorderly Youth in Public Places.** Michael S. Scott. 2001. ISBN: 1-932582-05-3
7. **Loud Car Stereos.** Michael S. Scott. 2001. ISBN: 1-932582-06-1
8. **Robbery at Automated Teller Machines.** Michael S. Scott. 2001. ISBN: 1-932582-07-X
9. **Graffiti.** Deborah Lamm Weisel. 2002. ISBN: 1-932582-08-8
10. **Thefts of and From Cars in Parking Facilities.** Ronald V. Clarke. 2002. ISBN: 1-932582-09-6
11. **Shoplifting, 2nd Edition.** Ronald V. Clarke. 2013. ISBN: 978-1-932582-34-5
12. **Bullying in Schools.** Rana Sampson. 2002. ISBN: 1-932582-11-8
13. **Panhandling.** Michael S. Scott. 2002. ISBN: 1-932582-12-6
14. **Rave Parties.** Michael S. Scott. 2002. ISBN: 1-932582-13-4
15. **Burglary of Retail Establishments.** Ronald V. Clarke. 2002. ISBN: 1-932582-14-2
16. **Clandestine Methamphetamine Labs, 2nd Edition.** Michael S. Scott and Kelly Dedel. 2006. ISBN: 1-932582-15-0
17. **Acquaintance Rape of College Students.** Rana Sampson. 2002. ISBN: 978-1-932582-00-2
18. **Burglary of Single-Family Houses.** Deborah Lamm Weisel. 2002. ISBN: 1-932582-17-7
19. **Misuse and Abuse of 911.** Rana Sampson. 2002. ISBN: 1-932582-18-5
20. **Financial Crimes Against the Elderly.** Kelly Dedel Johnson. 2003. ISBN: 1-932582-22-3
21. **Check and Card Fraud.** Graeme R. Newman. 2003. ISBN: 1-932582-27-4
22. **Stalking.** The National Center for Victims of Crime. 2004. ISBN: 1-932582-30-4
23. **Gun Violence Among Serious Young Offenders.** Anthony A. Braga. 2004. ISBN: 1-932582-31-2
24. **Prescription Drug Fraud and Misuse, 2nd Edition.** Julie Wartell and Nancy G. La Vigne. 2013. ISBN: 978-1-932582-37-6

51. **Pedestrian Injuries and Fatalities.** Justin A. Heinonen and John E. Eck. 2007. ISBN: 1-932582-83-5
52. **Bicycle Theft.** Shane D. Johnson, Aiden Sidebottom, and Adam Thorpe. 2008. ISBN: 1-932582-87-8
53. **Abandoned Vehicles.** Michael G. Maxfield. 2008. ISBN: 1-932582-88-6
54. **Spectator Violence in Stadiums.** Tamara D. Madensen and John E. Eck. 2008. ISBN: 1-932582-89-4
55. **Child Abuse and Neglect in the Home.** Kelly Dedel. 2010. ISBN: 978-1-935676-00-3
56. **Homeless Encampments.** Sharon Chamard. 2010. ISBN: 978-1-935676-01-0
57. **Stolen Goods Markets.** Michael Sutton. 2010. ISBN: 978-1-935676-09-6
58. **Theft of Scrap Metal.** Brandon R. Kooi. 2010. ISBN: 978-1-935676-12-6
59. **Street Robbery.** Khadija M. Monk, Justin A. Heinonen, and John E. Eck. 2010. ISBN: 978-1-935676-13-3
60. **Theft of Customers' Personal Property in Cafés and Bars.** Shane D. Johnson, Kate J. Bowers, Lorraine Gamman, Loreen Mamerow, and Anna Warne. 2010. ISBN: 978-1-935676-15-7
61. **Aggressive Driving.** Colleen Laing. 2010. ISBN: 978-1-935676-18-8
62. **Sexual Assault of Women by Strangers.** Kelly Dedel. 2011. ISBN: 978-1-935676-43-0
63. **Export of Stolen Vehicles Across Land Borders.** Gohar Petrossian and Ronald V. Clarke. 2012. ISBN: 978-1-935676-59-1
64. **Abandoned Buildings and Lots.** Jon M. Shane. 2012. ISBN: 978-1-932582-01-7
65. **Animal Cruelty.** Kelly Dedel. 2012. ISBN: 978-1-932582-05-5
66. **Missing Persons.** Kenna Quinet. 2012. ISBN: 978-1-932582-20-8
67. **Gasoline Drive-Offs.** Bruno Meini and Ronald V. Clarke. 2012. ISBN: 978-1-932582-15-4
68. **Chronic Public Inebriation.** Matthew Pate. 2012. ISBN: 978-1-932582-07-9
69. **Drug-Impaired Driving.** Joe Kuhns. 2012. ISBN: 978-1-932582-08-6
70. **Home Invasion Robbery.** Justin A. Heinonen and John E. Eck. 2013. ISBN: 978-1-932582-16-1
71. **Physical and Emotional Abuse of the Elderly.** Brian K. Payne. 2013. ISBN: 978-1-932582-67-3
72. **Hate Crimes.** Joshua D. Freilich and Steven M. Chermak. 2013. ISBN: 978-1-932582-78-9

Response Guides Series

1. **The Benefits and Consequences of Police Crackdowns.** Michael S. Scott. 2003. ISBN: 1-932582-24-X
2. **Closing Streets and Alleys to Reduce Crime: Should You Go Down This Road?** Ronald V. Clarke. 2004. ISBN: 1-932582-41-X
3. **Shifting and Sharing Responsibility for Public Safety Problems.** Michael S. Scott and Herman Goldstein. 2005. ISBN: 1-932582-55-X
4. **Video Surveillance of Public Places.** Jerry Ratcliffe. 2006. ISBN: 1-932582-58-4
5. **Crime Prevention Publicity Campaigns.** Emmanuel Barthe. 2006. ISBN: 1-932582-66-5
6. **Sting Operations.** Graeme R. Newman with assistance of Kelly Socia. 2007. ISBN: 1-932582-84-3
7. **Asset Forfeiture.** John L. Worall. 2008. ISBN: 1-932582-90-8
8. **Improving Street Lighting to Reduce Crime in Residential Areas.** Ronald V. Clarke. 2008. ISBN: 1-932582-91-6
9. **Dealing With Crime and Disorder in Urban Parks.** Jim Hilborn. 2009. ISBN: 1-932582-92-4
10. **Assigning Police Officers to Schools.** Barbara Raymond. 2010. ISBN: 978-1-935676-14-0
11. **Using Civil Actions Against Property to Control Crime Problems.** Martha J. Smith and Lorraine Mazerolle. 2013. ISBN: 978-1-932582-81-9

Problem-Solving Tools Series

1. **Assessing Responses to Problems: An Introductory Guide for Police Problem-Solvers.** John E. Eck. 2002. ISBN: 1-932582-19-3
2. **Researching a Problem.** Ronald V. Clarke and Phyllis A. Schultze. 2005. ISBN: 1-932582-48-7
3. **Using Offender Interviews to Inform Police Problem-Solving.** Scott H. Decker. 2005. ISBN: 1-932582-49-5
4. **Analyzing Repeat Victimization.** Deborah Lamm Weisel. 2005. ISBN: 1-932582-54-1
5. **Partnering with Businesses to Address Public Safety Problems.** Sharon Chamard. 2006. ISBN: 1-932582-62-2
6. **Understanding Risky Facilities.** Ronald V. Clarke and John E. Eck. 2007. ISBN: 1-932582-75-4
7. **Implementing Responses to Problems.** Rick Brown and Michael S. Scott. 2007. ISBN: 1-932582-80-0
8. **Using Crime Prevention Through Environmental Design in Problem-Solving.** Diane Zahm. 2007. ISBN: 1-932582-81-9

9. **Enhancing the Problem-Solving Capacity of Crime Analysis Units.** Matthew B. White. 2008. ISBN: 1-932582-85-1
10. **Analyzing Crime Displacement and Diffusion.** Rob T. Guerette. 2009. ISBN: 1-932582-93-2
11. **Analyzing and Responding to Repeat Offending.** Nick Tilley. 2013. ISBN: 978-1-932582-71-1
12. **Understanding Theft of 'Hot Products.'** Kate J. Bowers and Shane D. Johnson. 2013. ISBN: 978-1-932582-77-2

Special Publications

Crime Analysis for Problem Solvers in 60 Small Steps. Ronald V. Clarke and John E. Eck. 2005. ISBN:1-932582-52-5

Policing Terrorism: An Executive's Guide. Graeme R. Newman and Ronald V. Clarke. 2008.

Effective Policing and Crime Prevention: A Problem-Oriented Guide for Mayors, City Managers, and County Executives. Joel B. Plant and Michael S. Scott. 2009.

Implementing POP: Leading, Structuring, and Managing a Problem-Oriented Police Agency. Michael S. Scott and Stuart Kirby. 2012. ISBN: 978-1-932582-61-1

Intelligence Analysis for Problem Solvers. John E. Eck and Ronald V. Clarke. 2013. ISBN: 978-1-935676-55-3

Upcoming Problem-Oriented Guides for Police

Problem-Specific Guides
Robbery of Pharmacies

Problem-Solving Tools
Identifying and Defining Policing Problems

Response Guides
Monitoring Offenders on Conditional Release

For a complete and up-to-date listing of all available POP Guides, see the Center for Problem-Oriented Policing website at www.popcenter.org.

For more information about the *Problem-Oriented Guides for Police* series and other COPS Office publications, call the COPS Office Response Center at 800-421-6770, via e-mail at AskCopsRC@usdoj.gov, or visit COPS Online at www.cops.usdoj.gov.

www.ingramcontent.com/pod-product-compliance
Lightning Source LLC
Chambersburg PA
CBHW080852010626
R18376000001B/R183760PG45790CBX00014B/1